W O R L D   B A N K   W O R K I N G

New Technologies, New Risks?

Innovation and Countering the Financing of Terrorism

Andrew Zerzan

THE WORLD BANK
Washington, D.C.

World Bank Working Papers are published to communicate the results of the Bank's work to the development community with the least possible delay. The manuscript of this paper therefore has not been prepared in accordance with the procedures appropriate to formally-edited texts. Some sources cited in this paper may be informal documents that are not readily available.

ISBN-13: 978-0-8213-8086-4
eISBN: 978-0-8213-8177-9
ISSN: 1726-5878   DOI: 10.1596/978-0-8213-8086-4

Library of Congress Cataloging-in-Publication Data has been requested.

Contents

Tables

Figures

Boxcs

Foreword

Terrorism can endanger innocent human life and tear the very threads that hold society together, namely, trust and security. Governments have mobilized a variety of tools in response, ranging from the political to the economic. In attempting to prevent and detect terrorist financing and other forms of material support, those offering financial services have been required to heighten their vigilance of potential terrorist abuse of those services.

While protecting financial services from potential abuse, care should be taken not to deny access to those services to those most in need. Dejection and social exclusion are very often conducive to terrorism; therefore, ensuring inclusion of the disenfranchised and creating possibilities for their advancement is a key part of the broader, long-term struggle against terrorism and extremism. Expanding access to the financial system while promoting market integrity is critical to delivering real opportunities and relieving despair.

International standards and best practices on the fight against money laundering and terrorism financing have been developed over the past two decades. A review of the implementation and effectiveness of the standards on terrorism financing has recently been conducted under the aegis of the United Nations, with the World Bank playing a leading role. A recently published report, Tackling the Financing of Terrorism, by the UN Counter-Terrorism Implementation Task Force, made nearly a hundred recommendations on an array of terrorist financing issues, including new technologies, nonprofit organizations, informal remittance providers and international cooperation.

This paper addresses one of those recommendations, that the international community should promptly raise awareness of the risks, if any, of new technologies and practices for reducing them. We hope that it will bring useful insight to policy makers and practitioners as they work to protect their markets and communities from these terrorist threats while ensuring that the financial system works to facilitate economic development for the poor.

Consolate Rusagara
Director, Financial Systems
World Bank

Acknowledgments

This paper was created as a result of the World Bank's participation in the United Nations Counter Terrorism Implementation Task Force. This important brainstorming exercise provided access to many great minds in fields such as police, economics, law, intelligence, banking and finance as well as the workings of the international system. The opportunity to discuss, debate with, and listen to these many individuals made this paper possible. The substantive inputs and guidance by Emile van der Does and Jean Pesme (both from Financial Market Integrity, World Bank) are also especially appreciated.

The peer reviewers for this paper are: Dr. Thaer Sabri (E-Money Association), Sarah Rotman (Consultative Group to Assist the Poor), Emmanuel Mathias and Alain Vedrenne-Lacombe (both from the International Monetary Fund), Michael Defeo (United Nations Office on Drugs and Crime), David Murray (United States Treasury), and Carlo Corazza (Payment Systems, World Bank). Their comments and discussions before, during, and after the drafting greatly helped sharpen the paper and enlighten the author about their very diverse fields.

Lastly, the author would like to thank the following people and organizations for information provided or advice they shared about their experience in this field. Arvind Gupta, Wameek Noor, and Pierre-Laurent Chatain (all from the World Bank), Marina Solin (GSMA, a global mobile industry association), the U.S. Federal Reserve Bank of New York, Wayne Laramee (UK Financial Services Authority), Governor Sultan Al-Suwaidi (Central Bank of the United Arab Emirates), the E-Money Association, Arabinda Achayra (Nanyang University, Singapore), Sue Eckert (Brown University), Chady El-Khoury (International Monetary Fund), the Monetary Authority of Singapore, Horst Intscher (former director of Canada's Financial Intelligence Unit), and the U.S. Federal Bureau of Investigation.

Executive Summary

Recent developments in the way financial services are delivered have provided both opportunities for economic development and prompted fears of their attractiveness for crimes such as terrorist financing. This paper explores four innovations—value cards, mobile financial services, online banking/payments, and digital currencies—outlining how they work, analyzing their risks, and identifying some ways in which governments and providers are attempting to reduce their attractiveness to financiers of terrorism. Determining what the actual risks are is critical to ensuring that laws and regulations balance both the need to protect integrity in the market and to create an environment friendly to business and empowering to the poor.

Value Cards

One of the new mechanisms by which people can make a payment via a piece of plastic called a value card. These cards can be broken into two basic technology types: (i) centrally recorded value cards, in which the value of the card is stored in a main database; and (ii) unit value–recorded cards in which the value is kept on the card itself. The difference in the way the value is recorded is key to analysis of the terrorist financing risks and the measures for mitigating them. This is due to the location of the fund/activity records. Whether they are on the card or recorded elsewhere affects the ability of the operator or authorities to monitor account activity for criminal abuse.

Unit-recorded cards are declining in use and have a low level of interoperability outside a specified geography that has specialized retailers equipped to read the card. Their attractiveness to financiers of terrorist appears rather low. Centrally recorded value card technology, on the other hand, is growing in many parts of the globe. There is anecdotal evidence—but no known legal cases—that such cards have been used by terrorists to transfer funds because their value cannot be easily determined by customs and border control agents. However, the fact that these cards are centrally recorded has enabled the industry to develop tools that can help prevent their abuse such as activity monitoring systems and geographical limitations.

Mobile Financial Services

The very rapid and global boom of the mobile phone business has facilitated the expansion of another industry with great potential to enhance economic development, especially among the poor. Mobile financial services include ways to send and store money by using an existing bank account, opening a new account, or even bypassing a bank account altogether.

There are some inherent risks that these services carry yet it is the fact that providers are varied and are sometimes not overseen by authorities that may pose the greatest risk of their abuse for criminal purposes. At the same time, it is important to note that research did not find a single case of terrorist financing activity through mobile phone financial services to date. This positive sign is a reminder to policy makers moving forward: the regulation of mobile financial services should be based upon the risk they pose and not fear of the unknown.

Online Banking and Payments

Globally, about a fifth of the world uses the Internet with increasing numbers everywhere. Coinciding with the expansion of Internet usage is the adoption of online banking and payment services such as Internet banking and payments. While online banking goes through a bank account and therefore merely extends existing service, Internet payments do not. The latter are usually facilitated by nonbank financial intermediaries that generally do not make loans or deposits.

Internet banking does not seem to present a new or greater risk of being vulnerable to criminal abuse other than fraud, which is being tackled by the industry as fraud directly affects profitability. With this exception in mind, indications are that it presents challenges much the same as more conventional means of banking. On the other hand, online payments may pose a greater challenge because online payment providers sometimes fall outside the regulatory regime. This is often because providers in this industry are usually not banks and the government may not have enough time to catch up with the market. It is also the case that governments are at times unaware of such systems operating in their country. There is no evidence that either of these online financial services is inherently more attractive to terrorist financiers than other channels to transfer value.

Digital Currency

Distinct from other online banking and Internet payment systems, there exist complex, non-government-based units of value called digital currency—also known as digital precious metal because its value is linked to a valuable commodity such as gold. This currency is exchanged between account holders of the service. The systems exist outside of any one jurisdiction, making single government oversight impossible, and thus are a cause of concern. A recent case supports this apprehension because the largest provider of digital currency was prosecuted and pled guilty to charges that it was complicit in criminal financial abuse of its system, including money laundering.

At the same time, there is little reason to believe that digital currencies are attractive to terrorist financiers in particular. The systems have existed for several years and except for a single case (which remains undecided), research has not found any proof of their particular appeal to terrorist supporters. The international nature of digital currency systems demands the supervision of far more than a single national authority. Digital currency is vulnerable to lack of proper oversight. Since they are naturally multijurisdictional, governments should look toward developing criteria for determining supervisory responsibility.

Conclusion

The paper concludes that these new methods of payment do not offer particular usefulness to terrorist financiers. However, some of these channels could be attractive for general criminal abuse because they have an ambiguous place in the legal regime. Providers therefore, may not know about or elect to properly mitigate risks. The industry is encouraged to work within itself to share information to prevent and detect criminal activity. Governments should consult with industry in deciding regulation and industry should notify government prior to rolling out a new service. This will make government oversight more effective. Lastly, since many of these services are international in scope, government coordination and awareness raising is central.

Acronyms and Abbreviations

AML	anti-money laundering
CDD	customer due diligence
CFT	Combating the Financing of Terrorism
CTITF	United Nations Counter Terrorism Implementation Task Force
FATF	Financial Action Task Force on Money Laundering and Terrorist Financing
GSMA	GSM Association, the global mobile industry organization
KYC	"know your customer," rules for customer identification
m-FS	mobile phone financial services
POS	point of sale

Author's Biography

Andrew Zerzan analyzes technology as a key driver for sustainable economic development. At the World Bank, his work has focused on new innovations and their role in promoting access to financial services and market integrity. In 2006, Mr. Zerzan initiated published research on information and communication technologies for economic development at the World Bank Institute. His analysis has gauged the effectiveness of national and international regimes to mitigate the risks of growth, such as illicit money flows, terrorist financing, and money laundering. In 2008 he co-authored first-of-its-kind research on mobile banking in a report titled *Integrity in Mobile Phone Financial Services*, which separates the fact from the fiction on its risks. He was also part of the United Nations Counter Terrorism Implementation Task Force from 2007–2009, where he drafted and coordinated the global report called *Tackling the Financing of Terrorism*. Mr. Zerzan draws on his private sector experience as a consultant in Japan where he built a grassroots business that has bridged disparities in strategic communications among global companies. He was educated in the United Kingdom, Spain, Canada, and the United States. He is currently based in London, and can be reached at andrewzerzan@gmail.com.

CHAPTER 1

Introduction

Emerging Opportunities and Risks to the Markets

The rise of information and communication technologies in the past decades has facilitated major economic development. It has provided the poor with access to financial resources and prospects of a better life. This is especially true for technologies that give users the ability to electronically store and transfer funds. In many countries, it is no longer necessary to pay hefty fees to send money via a monopolistic bank or fear that the cash hidden under the bed be found by thieves. Innovations—from mobile phones in Asia and Africa to value cards in Latin America and Europe—have delivered an opportunity for the poor to overcome these barriers by lower costs, greater security, and other benefits just now being realized.

These technologies have even given tools to governments to detect and monitor criminal financial activity. Computers systems have been developed that can automatically flag and react to suspicious transactions, enabling authorities to better shield people and markets from abuses, ranging from petty fraud to terrorism. In sum, these new technologies offer great opportunities to improve and protect the lives of people everywhere.

In spite of this, the same innovations that can be used to detect and disrupt criminal activities have been implicated by some observers as buoying it.[1] Because new technological developments often arise without the knowledge of lawmakers, they can exist in an unregulated zone where "anything goes" that offers an opportunity for crime. Furthermore, there are concerns that fast-moving terrorist groups can take advantage of this unawareness to accomplish their insidious operations.[2]

The fear that these technologies can be used for crime and terrorism has led some governments to take a restrictive stance on their development, either by outright prohibition or by placing unnecessary limitations that renders the business unviable.[3] Ironically, these restrictions go against their end-goal, namely building a safer society because their expansion, ultimately, may reduce some of the factors that lead to terrorism. Therefore, technological advancement requires a constant vigilance on the part of policy makers, law enforcement, and intelligence to mitigate the risks of crimes such as terrorist financing but in a way that promotes their growth. It also requires that central banks, in their role as overseer of national payment systems, be given the capacity to adequately address such risks.

International Calls on the Issue

The traditional methods[4] through which financial transactions are initiated, processed, and settled are quickly being transformed by what the Financial Action Task Force[5] (FATF) calls "New Payment Methods." These are essentially technological advancements that allow transactions through innovative means. The most common are mobile phones, the Internet, and electronic cards. Each of these carries varying levels of opportunity as well as risk. Because of their newness, many have yet to be regulated or even fully considered by governments. This suggests that the financial transactions channeled through them can fall outside the financial regulatory umbrella, existing in a grey zone where rules of the game are not clear to the providers, potentially giving a window of opportunity to illicit activities, including terrorist financing.

Safe and sound regulation is important by bringing confidence to the markets. Poorly regulated financial channels can risk economic unsustainability.[6] Further, they may be abused for criminal conduct. Countries therefore have repeatedly called for more work to be done to explain these technologies and the risks they pose. Perhaps most notably, the United Nations General Assembly Review of the Counter-Terrorism Strategy in September 2008 called for the World Bank and International Monetary Fund to continue research into this field. Most recently, the UN Counter-Terrorism Implementation Task Force[7] called for such a study in its 2009 report titled *Tackling the Financing of Terrorism*.

Objective

This paper aims to begin answering these international calls. It provides an up-to-date description of how these new technologies work and what challenges jurisdictions face in dealing with the various new payment methods.

Secondly, the paper intends to evaluate the risks of these products, separating the fact from the fear of terrorist financing. It is hoped that by identifying the real risks, if any, governments can promote these services as a way to facilitate economic development in a safe and sound marketplace.

Layout of the Paper

Analytically one can distinguish four new platforms by which value can be transferred:

- value card systems
- mobile phone financial services (m-FS)
- online banking and payment services
- digital currency.

Although divided here for simplicity, these four channels can overlap each other and/or traditional financial services. This is especially so when a provider offers a variety of ways to access the same account. The following discussion will examine these technologies, their vulnerabilities to criminal abuse and terrorist financing, and the responses to mitigate them by governments and the industry itself.

Notes

[1] Demetis and Dyer 2006.

[2] For instance, see Ehrenfeld and Wood 2007.

[3] World Bank 2007b.

[4] This includes bank branches, ATMs, and conventional interfaces through traditional financial institutions.

[5] The Financial Action Task Force on Money Laundering and Terrorist Financing is the global standard-setter for anti-money laundering and counter-terrorist financing regimes. It has issued "Nine Special Recommendations on Terrorist Financing" on which countries are evaluated through regional bodies, the World Bank, the International Monetary Fund, and the FATF itself.

[6] Chatain et al. 2008.

[7] The United Nations Counter Terrorism Implementation Task Force (CTITF) is a multi-entity body to analyze the current approach to combating terrorism and possible ways to improve it. The report on "Tackling the Financing of Terrorism" was led by the World Bank, the IMF, and the UN Office on Drugs and Crime with the support of the UN Security Council's Al-Qaida/Taliban Monitoring Team, INTERPOL, and the UN Counter-Terrorism Executive Directorate.

CHAPTER 2

Value Card Systems

Prepaid cards, electronic purses, store gift cards, payroll cards, cash cards, phone cards and public transportation passes are all mechanisms by which people can pay for multiple or specific goods and services via a piece of plastic called a value card. These cards can be broken into two basic technology types:[1] (i) *centrally* recorded value cards, in which the value of the card is stored in a main database, that is, those that utilize a magnetic strip (such as those found on credit cards) or have a hidden printed number (often on phone cards) and; (ii) *unit* value recorded cards in which the value is kept on the card itself, that is, those that physically include a security-enabled memory microchip (such as a smart card).

The key difference between these two types of cards is where their value is logged. Centrally recorded value cards give users access to funds that have been recorded in a network or database of some kind.[2] The card merely contains the "log-on" data necessary to use it. For instance, a phone card may use a magnetic strip that he/she swipes or a printed secret number that the user dials into a phone to a faraway automated system to make long distance calls. Another example is a retailer's gift card, which usually has a magnetic strip that links the card to an account in the merchant's system. The customer uses the gift card to access the money stored in that account.[3]

Unit value recorded cards do not use a central database to keep track of the funds a customer has. These cards keep this information on the unit (that is, the card) itself through a computer chip that is within each card issued. This is similar to carrying money and therefore sometimes is called an electronic purse.

The difference in the way the value is recorded is key to analysis of the terrorist financing risks and the measures for mitigating them. This is due to the location of the fund/activity records. Whether it is on the card itself or recorded elsewhere affects the ability of the operator or authorities to monitor account activity for criminal abuse.

Centrally Recorded Value Cards

The use of centrally recorded value card is a booming business in many countries, especially among retailers.[4] Estimates of its present market size range from US$75 billion to over $155 billion with the U.S. share representing approximately half of the total.[5] They typically function similar to a debit card in that each card could be linked to an account or several cards are pooled in the same account. Accounts are held at various types of financial institutions but almost all pooled accounts are held at banks.[6]

Centrally recorded value cards can be categorized in two ways: those that are closed system and those that are open system, the difference being that closed are limited to a specific use/service/brand/location and open system are widely operable. Depending on the particular issuer, either open- or closed-system cards can be reused or "reloaded."[7]

Closed-system cards can be acquired and used anonymously in most cases. For terrorist financing, this can bring great opportunity as it provides cover for those wishing to transfer funds. Additionally, since the value of the card is stored in a centralized database, far from the card itself, it is difficult for authorities (or anyone beside the issuer for that matter) to determine its value upon inspection. Although these cards are generally unable to give users access to cash directly, they can be sold or the goods and services which they buy can be traded or sold.

These anonymity-providing characteristics have already been shown to be attractive to terrorist financiers in the past. Law enforcement authorities from two countries mentioned that there were cases under investigation in which terrorist financiers used large quantities of closed-system, centrally recorded value cards to move funds overseas.[8]

Open-system cards are generally associated with major credit/debit card providers such as Visa or MasterCard.[9] This gives the card the "open" trait because it can be used wherever such credit card brands are accepted although it may be restricted to certain regions. Although Visa and Mastercard use banks as an integral part of their business model, it is not technically necessary that open-system cards are linked to a bank account. Moreover, they can be, and often are, distributed by merchants and nonbank financial institutions. Customer acquisition and card issuance can occur either in person or through non-face-to-face means such as the Internet or telephone. The weakness of the system lies here. Open-system cards allow for easier traceability, due to their unique credit card-type number, but do not always mitigate the risks of anonymity. This is particularly relevant to prepaid cardholders who are not always properly identified at the initiation of the business relationship. This means that although the money trail can be followed, it may not be clear who the real user is. Money can be withdrawn from ATMs in foreign jurisdictions and used for criminal means.

Some measures have been identified to mitigate the risks of centrally recorded value cards.[10] These include requiring issuers to perform proper due diligence requirements for transactions above certain levels, based on the risk that certain cumulative transaction levels would pose. This would help mitigate the risks of anonymity posed by this new payment method. Furthermore, setting certain limits based on geography or transaction amount could also be a way to reduce the attractiveness of this technology being used for criminal means. Since these cards are often issued to specific market segments (teenagers, adults without a bank account, etc), it is possible that such measures could be taken without damaging the business. An example of this is the American centrally recorded card issuer, Green Dot, which has already taken such measures.

Figure 2.1. Centrally Recorded and Unit-Recorded Value Card Setup

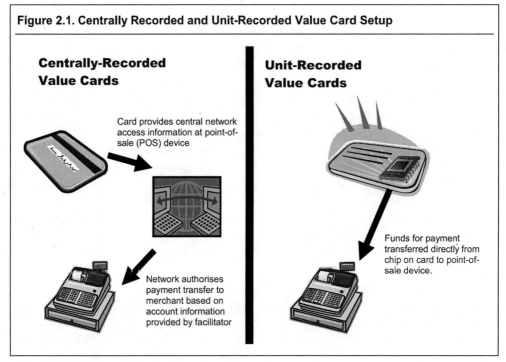

Source: World Bank analysis of value card models.

Unit Recorded Value Cards

Unit recorded value cards are much like cash in that the card is the storage place of funds available. The overall dispersion of such cards is rather low, mainly because centrally recorded value cards hold multi-purpose potential and unit recorded ones usually do not. There have even been efforts in some countries to fuse the two into one single card but there has been little success in market adoption of these combined cards or unit recorded value cards alone.[11]

These cards may or may not require activation through a financial institution, nor do they necessarily require one to withdraw, "reload," or deposit funds into the card. Users are often anonymous because countries generally do not require customer due diligence measures to be taken and often issuers do not find a business reason to record them.[12]

This type of value card does not have inherent limits on how much money can be stored; however, due to the limited nature of these cards (public transportation, parking passes, and so forth), they are used for small transactions with one or just a few merchants. This makes issuers put low limits on the total amount permitted on the card at one time. For instance, one of the most widely used unit recorded value cards is Proton (Belgium) which limits the user to a maximum account balance[13] of €125. This is similar to other cards of this category.

As other new payment methods emerge and evolve, it seems unlikely that unit value recorded cards will play a significant factor in the market. Equipment costs, lack of interoperability and of a uniform network hinder market adoption and so many issuers are dropping the service altogether. Northern Europe is perhaps the largest market for such cards yet even there the future prospects seem dim.[14]

Summary

General

The two major types of value card systems, one that centrally records the value and one that records it on the cards itself, bring entirely different levels of risk of criminal abuse.[15] Additionally, the growth of the former and decline of market share of the latter implies that regulatory attention should be prioritized.

That some of these value card systems offer anonymity to a greater degree than traditional payment methods could play a role in making them more attractive to criminals. Measures have been taken at uneven degrees by issuers that have mitigated these risks in some value card brands but certainly not all.

To ensure that providers fall under the AML/CFT regulatory regime, it is essential that countries recognize that value cards are monetary instruments and/or financial products[16] and should therefore be subject to laws governing such. The legal ambiguity of the electronic monies kept in value cards has been cited by a number of experts as the central reason for the weakness of regulatory measures to deal with their risks.[17] This action would significantly strengthen law enforcement efforts to curb abuse of value cards without seriously hampering their benefits to the market.

Terrorist Financing

Implementing controls for cross-border physical currency movements[18] to mitigate the risks of terrorist financing could very well be a challenge for value cards that are bearer negotiable (which is the case for unregistered prepaid cards). There is anecdotal evidence that centrally recorded value cards have been used by terrorists to move transfer funds because their value cannot be easily determined by customs and border control agents. However, the very fact that these cards are centrally recorded has enabled the industry to develop tools that can help prevent their abuse. As noted earlier, the geographic limitations put on these cards are one such measure that seems well targeted to mitigate cross-border criminal risks, including terrorist financing.

Unit-recorded cards seem very unlikely to be attractive to terrorist funding operations. They lack interoperability and are quite limited in both account balance and geography. The limited nature of the card also hinders cross-border movements of currency.[19] The FATF calls this "significant" in reducing the risk that these cards will be used for terrorist financing and therefore has not observed either money laundering or terrorist financing typologies of this new payment method.[20]

Notes

[1] The terms here are from the authors based on research into money card-based technologies. For more information see CPSS (2003) and Evaluation Partnership Limited (2006).
[2] The funds themselves are often stored in a pooled bank account but the tracking of each cardholder's money is on the card operator's network.
[3] Based on World Bank research into various value card schemes.

[4] World Bank field work: Deloitte and Touche. "Gift Cards, Money Laundering, and Fraud: Protecting Against the Perfect Holiday Storm." Consumer Business Webcast. 13 December 2007. Speakers include: David Gilles, Stacy Janiak, Brian Midkiff and John Scheffler.

[5] Yingling 2007. Lower figure based on discussions with John Scheffler, U.S. Assurance Leader, Retail, Deloitte & Touche USA LLP in December 2007.

[6] See FATF 2006.

[7] See Furletti 2004.

[8] World Bank field work and Deloitte and Touche 2007.

[9] For further discussion on this card-type see FATF 2006.

[10] NBPCA 2007.

[11] The Evaluation Partnership Limited 2006.

[12] World Bank research in the field.

[13] European Committee for Banking Standards 2003.

[14] The Evaluation Partnership Limited 2006.

[15] "Hybrid" cards have also emerged. These cards store money on both the card itself and on a central server, which may allow the user to have the benefits of unit-recorded cards while being protected from fraud.

[16] The terms "financial product" and "monetary instrument" have distinct meanings depending on the jurisdiction. In the United States, for instance, "monetary instrument" implies that the physical transfer of the instrument is the transfer of ownership while "financial product" carries a broader meaning.

[17] World Bank field work and Deloitte and Touche 2007.

[18] FATF Special Recommendation IX

[19] Albeit the euro has brought opportunities to issuers of these cards to enable them with cross-border capabilities.

[20] See FATF 2006.

CHAPTER 3

Mobile Phone Financial Services

The rapid dispersion of mobile technology in the past decade is far reaching, with over three billion users today worldwide.[1] Although many developed economies have market penetration[2] of over 100 percent, the growth is bound to continue with new wireless networks being built in poorer regions. Moreover, in 2006 mobile phones became the first communications technology to have more users in the developing world than the developed world;[3] more than 60 percent of all subscribers are now located in developing countries.[4]

The spread of mobile technology has been accompanied by an evident deepening of the market itself. Subscribers are demanding more services from their phones while technology and providers are quickly moving to offer it. This is particularly true in the case of mobile phone financial services (m-FS). These services are being developed in a number of countries with the most advanced business models prevalent in East Asia and Southern Africa. These business models can vary from a telecom company merely passing on information from a financial institution to providing mobile currency in the form of airtime credits. A brief summary of these services is presented in the following sections.

Figure 3.1. Surge in Mobile Connections across All Regions

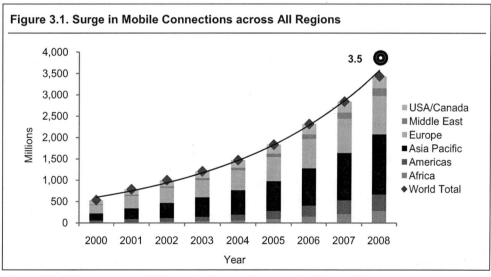

Source: World Bank analysis of Wireless Intelligence Data provided March 2008.
Note: Figure shows millions of mobile connections regionally (bars) and worldwide (line). First quarter figures, Q1 from 2000 to 2008.

Mobile Financial Information

Mobile phone financial services are often initially provided in the form of mobile financial information as a way for telecom companies to test the market demand for such services. Mobile financial information generally includes account balance data, transaction records and securities quotes. For this analysis, the importance of mobile financial information lies in the fact that, in developing countries, it is a bellwether for more advanced m-FS.

Mobile Bank and Securities Account

Perhaps the m-FS that is most commonly understood is that which allows customers to access their bank account. The service empowers customers to pay bills, transfer money between bank accounts, and settle credit card invoices all though a mobile phone (by sending a text message or through software). It allows access anytime and anywhere there is a wireless signal, which is growing ever more ubiquitous. In a variety of countries mobile bank account services have been launched and can be complemented by those that permit securities transactions.[5] The characteristic that defines this service is that it is anchored in an account provided by a bank or securities firm.

Although the mobile bank and securities account service is anchored in accounts managed through traditional financial institutions, customers may interface with the telecom company directly in accessing account services. Moreover, in some instances the customer may not even realize his/her relation to a bank or securities firm at all. This may be the result of the strong coordination between banking and telecom providers, which at times can be so tight that the telecom is recognized as a "branch" of the bank.[6] Even though the service may be regulated as a joint-venture, the customer will deal only directly with the telecom.

Bank and securities firms are generally regulated entities under the FATF 40+9 framework. As such, mobile bank and securities accounts are aptly acknowledged by the FATF[7] as an extension of traditional retail electronic payment systems and therefore pose little or no greater risk than the traditional services to which they extend access. This implies that it is no more *inherently* risky than traditional methods. However, *exogenous* factors such as its place in the regulatory regime can have a profound effect on the level of risk the service actually poses. This caveat is the crux of risk analysis of new technologies and will be discussed later in this chapter.

Mobile Payment

In some cases, nontraditional financial institutions facilitate transactions through mobile phones. In fact, such business models are growing increasingly popular as telecom operators and others[8] are running their own m-FS without anchoring each account with a bank or securities firm. Such non-traditional financial institutions provide what are called mobile payments. Their emergence has been seen in a variety of markets including Africa, Latin America, and East Asia with many more to follow.[9]

Mobile payments are celebrated for carrying great potential for economic development. Their independence from traditional financial institutions frees them from certain limitations,[10] possibly making them more powerful in expanding access to financial services, a key to market growth and deepening.[11] This potential has prompted particular pressure to keep the way clear for mobile payment services to flourish without being greatly burdened by government.

As mobile financial information does not enable users to perform transactions, it is not directly vulnerable in and of itself. It could be used, however, as a means to deter terrorist financing-related crimes due to its facilitation of detection. The convenience and speed by which users can monitor their accounts allows for quick detection of illicit transactions. In the case of the other m-FS, certain risk factors exist.

Recent analysis[12] has revealed that m-FS that allow transactions, such as mobile payments and mobile bank and securities accounts, are vulnerable to four major risk factors. Inherent risks of these services include anonymity, elusiveness and rapidity and poor oversight, which, while not a danger in itself, can aggravate any of the other three.

Anonymity and Elusiveness

Various m-FS products such as mobile bank and securities accounts and mobile payments may pose a heightened risk of customer anonymity if proper systems are not in place. There are a number of ways this can happen. In some countries, prepaid mobile users are not required to register their phones with the provider so the identity of the user is unknown. As m-FS become more prevalent, there is concern that terrorist financiers could take advantage of this to send money while hiding its source.

Additionally, the use of false identification could allow for the same problem. The nature of m-FS is such that identity may only be verified in a face-to-face manner at the purchase of the phone and subsequent usage will be remote and without the use of identification normally required for traditional transactions done in-person at a bank branch. The possibility that a registered user could hand over his/her phone to criminals to use for illicit activity or that the phone would be stolen for such use could pose a real danger. In some countries this has already been seen amongst criminal organizations for drug trafficking purposes.[13]

Another concern is "smurfing," which is the use of small transactions to hide the greater sum that ultimately is being transferred. This could provide anonymity for the criminal. Furthermore, the fact that m-FS transaction costs are significantly lower than other methods of moving funds are an additional incentive to use this channel to move money.

It is very much in this context that a second risk factor, elusiveness, may exist in the use of m-FS to facilitate money movements. Certain cultural practices could provide cover for the true initiator and recipient of a transaction. Mobile phone "pooling" use in poorer communities and the delegation of use in wealthier circles are both examples of this.

Phone pooling is a growing practice in rural villages throughout Africa and Asia. The local community appoints a responsible person to manage a mobile phone that is shared among those in the village. If the phone is registered, it will be under the name of the responsible carrier, not all of those in the community

Wealthier communities sometimes practice a custom of phone delegation. In this situation, the wealthy person authorizes another individual to act on their behalf in managing the phone. The phone may be legally registered to the wealthy person but is never used directly by them. This practice could be abused for illicit financial activity if the authorized agent misuses the phone to avoid customer profiling. In some countries, as will be discussed later, financial institutions, law enforcement and financial intelligence units profile customer activity. This is also true in some markets for m-FS. A large transaction may appear consistent the profile of the wealthy individual to whom the phone is registered, even though that person is unaware that the authorized agent is clandestinely working as an intermediary for criminal activity. The transfer is unlikely to be flagged by authorities because its size is not inconsistent with the customer profile of the wealthy individual.

Rapidity

The convenience of m-FS, that they can be used virtually anywhere at any time and quickly, can facilitate efforts to "layer" a transaction. In money laundering terminology, layering refers to the practice of obscuring the origin of funds by complicating its path (for example, transferring them frequently through different accounts and preferably from/to different jurisdictions). The low costs and high speed at which this can be done allows for layering to occur in a much easier way than traditional transfer methods which can require face-to-face interaction with bank personnel at each step. A criminal could easily move the funds across multiple m-FS accounts by sitting in the same spot with several phones in hand.

Poor Oversight

The foremost risk that m-FS products carry is that they will fall outside the regulations in some countries. This means that the AML/CFT regulations in place for other financial institutions may not legally apply to the new providers that facilitate m-FS (such as telecom companies) because their primary business is not the provision of financial services but something else (such as telecommunications). Since in many countries the m-FS market is generally newer than the AML and CFT legislation, governments did not consider them or their providers when drafting those laws. This factor can exacerbate the three inherent risks above because providers will not be detected and sanctioned for unsafe practices as traditional financial institutions are for non-compliance with AML/CFT procedures.

Further complicating the problem is determining the right government authority to oversee m-FS. Governments may elect to regulate these businesses through their ministry of communication or technology, which may not have the mandate or the tools to oversee it. In cases where a bank is involved, there is often confusion for which AML/CFT controls each party is responsible (for instance, if there is a bank account linked to the m-FS service, which party is legally responsible for the AML/CFT controls, the telecom or the bank?). Countries that have regulated m-FS do not demonstrate a consistent framework for others to follow in this regard. Some jurisdictions put the onus of AML/CFT on the bank while others shift it to a greater degree to the telecom. This is even true within jurisdictions where one type of m-FS is regulated differently than another.

Mitigation of the Risks

Although not all countries have responded to m-FS in their markets, there are a number of measures in effect in various jurisdictions. These include: specially set Know-Your-Customer procedures, advanced identification mechanisms, limits on transaction amounts, customer profiling, monitoring and internal controls, centralized registries of account holders, guidelines on AML/CFT and licensing for m-FS providers.

Know-Your-Customer (KYC)[14] tailored to m-FS

In response to the need to acquire customers by off-branch or non-face-to-face procedures, some jurisdictions have adopted alternative verification measures. The main procedures implemented are (i) legal exceptions to verifying customer's residential address during initiation of the banking relationship (so long as transactions do not exceed prescribed limits), (ii) alternative verification methods, and (iii) restricted functionality. Rather than via face-to-face contact, customer identification is established by cross-checking customer information with third party databases, such as a national tax or social insurance databases, or other reliable sources like a telecom's database of active customers. Telecoms register customers for m-FS using mobile phones and the Internet, but these customers are restricted to basic transactions until they have a face-to-face screening.

A new development that facilitates KYC measures is that of mandatory SIM card (the unique chip inside the phone) registration. For instance, the telecommunications regulator in Côte d'Ivoire has set a deadline for mobile operators to identify all users of its cellular network.[15] This practice would greatly reduce the risk of anonymity and aid in monitoring accounts for criminal activity.

Innovative Mechanisms for Identification

The security of the mobile telephone device itself combined with personal passwords provides two deterrents to protect against unauthorized m-FS users. Fieldwork also revealed use of more advanced measures like biometric authentication and electronic signature (e-signature) to complete financial transactions. To ensure that the costs of such technology are not borne by local retailers (which could impede its adoption in poorer communities) biometric authentification mechanisms are sometimes applied in a centralized way. This means that the advanced biometric technology is based at the company's headquarters rather than spread over multiple agents. A provider in South Africa, for instance, has tested a biometric voice identification system for m-FS.[16]

Innovative KYC does not always imply a technological solution. For instance, one provider[17] has trained hundreds of local agents who verify customers' identities at their homes. This can solve KYC challenges in places where local communities do not have identification cards or live in remote locations.

Transaction Amount Limits

Limited transaction amounts and imposed reporting thresholds are the most popular control measures adopted by regulators and the private sector. The lack of data available on m-FS means that transaction limits have been set rarely as a result of risk-based analysis.[18] Instead, limits for m-FS transactions were set arbitrarily at levels similar to those for other channels, such as ATMs or the Internet. In the Republic of Korea, however, limits have been set based on statistical analysis of the number and magnitude of transactions (see box 3.1).

Customer Profiling

Providers of m-FS in some locations have developed systems to monitor customer activities against their profiles by highlighting unusual transaction patterns. Profiles are built based on information provided at the time of customer acquisition and are modified on an ongoing basis. Data collected includes customer income level, transaction history, and services and channels frequently used. One advantage of customer profiling is that it does not require sophisticated software or complex IT rules.

Monitoring and Internal Controls

The same technology that enables m-FS is also used by providers to moderate their exposure to risk. Unlike only using manual controls, which usually require time and recurring human intervention, bank, telecom and other m-FS providers enhance manual controls with automated ones embedded in IT systems. This is particularly relevant to AML/CFT measures as automated controls can quickly scan the name, date of birth, etc. and compare with the various UN terrorism list and others of its kind.

Box 3.1. Risk-based Determination of Transaction Limits

The Case of the Republic of Korea

Electronic funds transfer law and supervisory regulations have established limits on transactions conducted using mobile bank and securities accounts in Korea. The limits are based on a statistical analysis of the volume, frequency, and other data gathered by the Financial Supervisory Services. Transaction amounts (in Korean won) are grouped into three categories that fall under increasingly stringent security measures relative to the transaction amount. Financial institutions may also apply greater security controls based on the preference of the customer.

Number of transactions

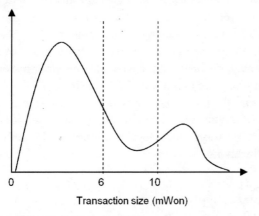

Category 1: W 0–6 million (US$6,000). Constitutes 85% of all transactions.

Category 2: W 6–10 million (US$10,000). Constitutes 5% of all transactions.

Category 3: W >10 million (>US$10,000). Constitutes 10% of all transactions.

Transaction size (mWon)

Source: World Bank field work (2008).

Centralized Registry of Account Holders

A centralized registry of account holders to prevent abuse of users with multiple m-FS accounts is being contemplated in some jurisdictions. Through a central repository, telecom operators and regulators would view suspicious activity by transfers associated with a name, not solely an account number. Presuming there are sufficient controls to mitigate anonymity risks, law enforcement and telecoms could use this database to find multiple accounts tied to the same user. This would help hinder criminal efforts to conceal the origins of funds by taking advantage of the lack of information shared within the industry.

The Issuance of Guidelines

In one country, the government published AML/CFT guidelines for companies entering the m-FS market. This ensures that providers know their responsibilities and closes any regulatory holes from lack of uncertainty.

Supervision/Licensing/Registration of m-FS Providers

FATF Recommendation 23 stresses the need for jurisdictions to have proper licensing processes for financial institutions and is amplified by Special Recommendation VI: "Each country should take measures to ensure that … legal entities, including agents, that provide a service for the transmission of money or value, including transmission through an informal money or value transfer system or network should be licensed or registered and subject to all the FATF Recommendations that apply to banks and nonbank financial institutions." Procedures to ensure that m-FS providers, including telecom companies, are acting with proper authorization exist in some of the markets where it has taken off. This will ensure that the business is adequately applying AML/CFT controls.

Summary

General

As the growth of mobile phones continues to affect all regions of the world, it is becoming increasingly important for governments to deal with the criminal vulnerabilities posed by m-FS and take advantage of the potential it has to deter crime. Worldwide numbers for m-FS will reach over a billion users in the coming years (see figure 3.2).

In some ways, m-FS may be effective in fighting fraud.[19] Mobile Financial Information services can flag account activity to the user via the mobile phone. Should there be unauthorized access to a bank account, the user can be notified immediately.

However, m-FS do pose some inherent criminal risks: anonymity, elusiveness, and rapidity. These risks have been unevenly mitigated by countries using the techniques explained above. Yet it is that unevenness that causes concern. The fact that many, if not most, countries have not developed a regulatory regime to oversee the implementation of the measures necessary to mitigate these risks could allow the technology to be used for criminal purposes.

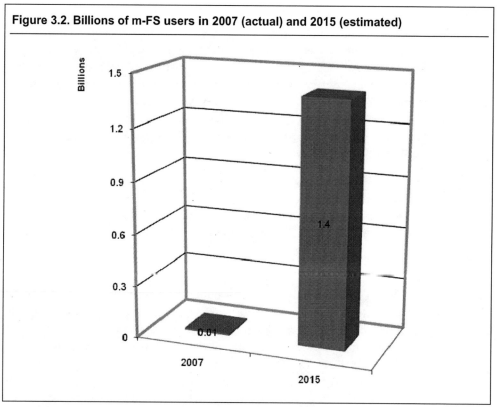

Figure 3.2. Billions of m-FS users in 2007 (actual) and 2015 (estimated)

Source: Global mobile industry association commissioned report (GSMA).

Among the various types of m-FS, criminal risks associated with mobile payments may be higher in some countries than mobile bank and securities accounts due to the ease by which funds can be moved across national borders. Settlement of international mobile payments may not always go through the same clearing systems that are necessary for those of traditional financial institutions. For instance, a cross border funds transfer through a mobile payment service may be lumped together with others so intermediary financial institutions and authorities, such as the central bank, only see one large transaction under the name of the m-FS provider. Information on the identity of the sender or receiver of the actual transactions may only be kept in the telecom's records and not be immediately accessible, as generally would be the case in traditional wire transfers.[20] This could be exploited by criminals. Coupled with the risks of mobile digital currencies,[21] such as cash-transferable airtime credit, the risks of the service could be relatively higher than traditional methods of transferring value.

Terrorist Financing

The practice of phone pooling can present a risk that the registered user is not the one initiating a transaction. This poses a general criminal risk, not one specific to terrorist financing.

As noted above, the fact that m-FS may allow criminals to "smurf" their transactions could make it more vulnerable to abuse. This may be particularly relevant to terrorist financing as terrorist fund requirements are generally lower than other financial crimes. This is illustrated by what is known of the 9/11 terrorist attack preparations. The funding provided to the perpetrators appears to have been sent in much smaller transfers than what is normal for other crimes (laundering the profits from narcotrafficking for example). It is for this reason that proper monitoring and effective KYC measures are considered and implemented by the provider.

At the same time, it is important to note that research did not find a single case of terrorist financing activity through mobile phone financial services. This positive sign is a reminder to policy makers moving forward: m-FS should be regulated based upon the risk they pose and not upon fear.

The worry on the part of policy makers that regulation of m-FS could hinder the market's development seems unsupported by industry practices. Many m-FS providers, however unintentionally, already take the CFT measures necessary to mitigate the risks even though they are not required to do so under the law. Apparently, many such practices are an important part of good business and therefore would not hinder access to financial services anymore than market forces themselves. In order to gain the political will to regulate the industry it will be increasingly necessary for this to be known. The objectives of CFT and economic development are aligned.

Notes

[1] Fieldwork, analysis and data for this section were based to a large extent on Chatain et al. 2008.

[2] Mobile market penetration is defined as the percent of the population with a mobile phone. Penetration over 100 percent implies that some users have more than one phone (for example, one for business and another for personal use).

[3] GSM Association 2006.

[4] ITU 2007.

[5] For instance in Korea, stock trading is available through a mobile phone account.

[6] In such instances the customer's information is verified by the telecom but a banking account is opened.

[7] See FATF 2006.

[8] In some countries, non-telecom, nonbank financial institutions are engaging in mobile payment schemes.

[9] Western Union extended its service to over 800 million mobile phone users in 2008. See Western Union Press Release "Western Union and GSMA to Create New Global Mobile Money Transfer Service," http://ir.westernunion.com/press/releaseDetail.cfm?ReleaseID=269902.

[10] Costs, regulations, and negative perceptions by some low-income groups which are thus resistant to engaging them in business.

[11] For a number of reasons including increased competition in the financial sector. See World Bank 2007a for more on this subject.

[12] Chatain et al. 2008.

[13] In Brazil for instance these accounts are called "orange accounts" in which drug dealers have the impoverished open a mobile payment account in their name, thus hiding the true user.

[14] KYC is the due diligence and bank regulation that financial institutions and other regulated entities must perform to identify their clients and ascertain relevant information pertinent to doing financial business with them.

[15] Discussion with Sarah Rotman (Consultative Group to Assist the Poor) on her fieldwork to the region in spring 2009.

[16] MTN Banking, a division of the Standard Bank of South Africa.

[17] Whizzit in South Africa

[18] Another approach is a point-based KYC approach. This system presumes that the more KYC evidence a customer is able to provide (national ID, driver's license, passport, physical presence, and so forth), the more the customer can be trusted so services are offered proportionally to identification provided.

[19] Since users can set their mobile phone to receive regular transaction confirmations, mobile financial information services can be used to more quickly detect fraudulent access to an account.

[20] Information based on interviews with World Bank Payment Systems Unit (March 2008)

[21] Still yet to be rolled out as of the publication of this paper.

CHAPTER 4

Online Banking and Payment Services

The explosion in Internet usage is impressive—almost one in five people now use the Internet worldwide. Observers around the globe hail it as an important development to improve the lives of the poor, strengthen good governance, and enhance human rights. This has put substantial pressure on governments to keep it free from unnecessary supervision. The American government even has in place a moratorium on taxes on access charges to promote its continued expansion.[1]

Coinciding with the expansion of Internet usage is the adoption of online banking and payment services such as Internet banking and Internet payments. While online banking goes through a bank and therefore merely extends existing service, Internet payments do not. The latter are facilitated by nonbank financial intermediaries that generally do not make loans or deposits.

Figure 4.1. Internet Boom across Regions 1990–2005 (users per thousand people)

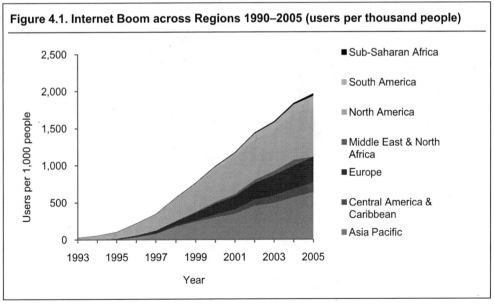

Source: Author's analysis of data provided by the International Telecommunications Union (1990 to 2005) (www.itu.int) and the World Resources Institute (www.wri.org).
Note: 2005 data for the Middle East and North Africa was unavailable at the time of publication.

Both of these services are growing quickly around the world. Although the ratio of users in the population is higher in developed countries, there is still a significant market in developing countries. Full statistics on global use of both of these services are not available because there has not been a full study on the level of online payment and banking services use in each country. However, Figure 4.2 is a sample comparison that demonstrates these online services are significant in both developed and developing countries.

Internet Banking[2]

Internet or online banking allows users to access their bank accounts without physically going to the bank itself. It also brings convenience as customers are able to view an array of account information and banking services typically requiring in-house customer service. These services include cheque deposits, securities purchases, bill settlements, funds transfers and even credit card and loan applications and authorizations. The growth of banking of this kind is likely to expand as more banks offer their services through the Internet.[3]

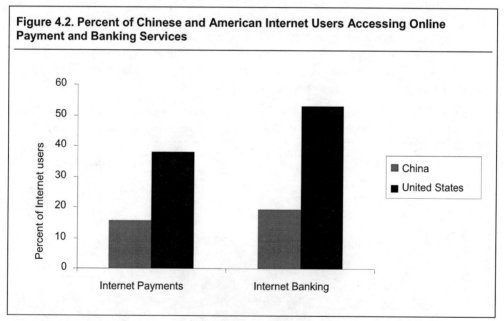

Figure 4.2. Percent of Chinese and American Internet Users Accessing Online Payment and Banking Services

Source: World Bank Analysis of statistics.
China data: China Internet Network Information Centre (CNNIC). 2008. *Statistical Survey Report on the Internet Development in China.* January. http://www.cnnic.net.cn/uploadfiles/pdf/2008/2/29/104126.pdf.
United States data: Pew Internet and American Life Project. 2007. "Internet Activities." Statistic for banking from survey data in September 2007. Statistic for payments from survey data from January 2005. http://www.pewInternet.org/trends/Internet_Activities_2.15.08.htm.

In the past decade there have been calls by standard-setters and regulatory bodies for enhanced vigilance over this channel. For instance, the AML/CFT assessment of the United States says, "the Federal Banking Agencies recognize electronic banking as a higher risk area." The reasons for this are similar to some of those noted above on m-FS, anonymity in particular. Banks, in an effort to reduce their exposure to criminal abuses such as fraud (which can severely damage their business), have increasingly developed systems to mitigate fraud risks. Multi-factor identification mechanisms are a common method for example. Users in many online banks must provide their password *in addition to* some other personal information,[4] asked at random, to login to many banks' websites. The success of these systems at ensuring a user is whom he says he is, is indicated by the rapid adoption of these methods by banks around the globe.[5]

Internet Payments

Nonbank financial institutions are increasingly facilitating transactions. This is true both on more traditional channels—Western Union for instance—and on the Internet. The most famous of these online providers is Paypal, an American company[6] that holds nearly 200 million online accounts[7] in 17 different currencies and is accessible in most countries.[8] Internet payment systems such as this allow users to transfer funds without the need of a bank for peer-to-peer transfers. However, it is common to deposit funds into the system or take funds out of the system through a traditional financial institution.

Internet payment providers may require that recipients of funds transfers link their account to a bank account or credit card at start up. This prerequisite for service is intended to verify customer identification to reduce the financial institution's exposure to fraud and other commercial risks.[9] It is also a tool against other criminal abuse because it requires that customers clear the same initial due diligence needed for regular bank account opening. Also, due to the nature of online transactions, it is often necessary—or at least simpler—to use traditional financial services to bring funds into the Internet payment system. This has given watchful providers a way to recognize potentially suspicious transactions.

At the same time, ongoing monitoring of customer activity through Internet payment systems may be different than that of a bank due to the level of regulation in the industry. Internet payment providers may not be fully incorporated into the regulatory regime of a country, something that holds true for other new technologies as well.[10] This could mean that the nonbank financial institution is not implementing all or any of the proper monitoring, detection and reporting practices that banks do, leaving a gap in the regulatory umbrella through which illicit funds could flow.[11]

Fieldwork[12] reveals that the speed at which such transactions take place can buoy criminals' efforts to hide the origin of funds. This can pose a significant risk if not mitigated properly.[13] This is because it allows quick transfers of funds, facilitating efforts to complicate (and ultimately render untraceable) their movements if not monitored through proper record keeping. It can also hinder efforts to seize the funds once they have been identified as illicit because they can be moved out before freezing or confiscation measures are implemented.

Box 4.1. Indicators of Internet Payment System Crime

The FATF has cited some "red-flags" of criminal abuse of Internet payment accounts:

- The customer opens his individual Internet account with the payment service provider in one country but logs in regularly on the website from a single or multiple third countries.
- The account opened by the customer is loaded with funds transferred from a third country, which could indicate that the customer does not live in the country from which he registered but in another country where he cannot register.
- The customer loads his Internet account with cash, if the Internet payment services provider allows loading with cash.
- The customer purchases items of high value or purchases middle-high-value items on a regular basis with a prepaid debit card, an anonymous prepaid credit card, or a gift card where the origin of the funds is difficult to retrace.
- The buyer requests that the goods be delivered to a post office box or to a different address from the one registered to the account (facilities depending on the country of destination).
- A customer opens an account with an Internet payment service provider, loads the account with important amounts of money, leaves the funds on the account during a certain period of time, and requests the redemption of the funds later on.
- The use of credit cards, particularly prepaid, issued in a foreign country.
- Abnormality with the proposed price on an auction site or during an auction sale indicating a possible complicity between buyer and seller (a customer offers to purchase an item at a price largely higher than the requested price). Additional factors could include multiple transactions between the same buyers and sellers.
- The purchased goods are regularly shipped to a foreign country.
- The customer uses a credit card issued by a bank in an offshore center or in a FAFT non-cooperative country.

Source: FATF 2008.

A second issue is that until recently there were very few systems effectively mitigating the risk of stolen information being used to fraudulently open an Internet payment account for illicit purposes. If a bank client's name and bank account number are used to open a fake Internet payment account, the client may not be able to detect it since it is unlikely that the client will be notified that there was ever a verification of their bank account.

There are efforts to mitigate this risk however, by authenticating a requestor of an Internet payment account by non-Internet means. For instance, before an account opening is authorized, the Internet payment provider may use an automated system to call the user's registered phone number. The user is then asked to answer a few basic personal questions to identify him/herself. Another method is to make a small deposit into a user's bank account and have the user verify the amount. Alternatively, a user may be required to confirm delivery of a letter by post with an authorization code. This validates a physical location and can reduce the risk of online fraud.

Verifying an address can also be used to set certain limitations to use. In fact, some Internet payment providers already do this by restricting functionality based on geographic location. One Internet payment provider does not allow for persons in riskier[14] jurisdictions to withdraw cash from their account. Clients in these locations may only make purchases and deposits with the funds in their Internet payment account. This measure is particularly targeted to reduce the risk of illicit uses of the system such as terrorist financing.

For customers that do have access to withdrawal services, some providers use a risk-based transaction limit scheme. Moneybookers Ltd, a British Internet payments provider,[15] increases its 90-day transaction limit depending on how the user verifies his name. If it is confirmed via a credit card, the limit is raised significantly but not as much as if verified through a bank account. It has a separate limit for users who wish to only verify their address through the method described above.

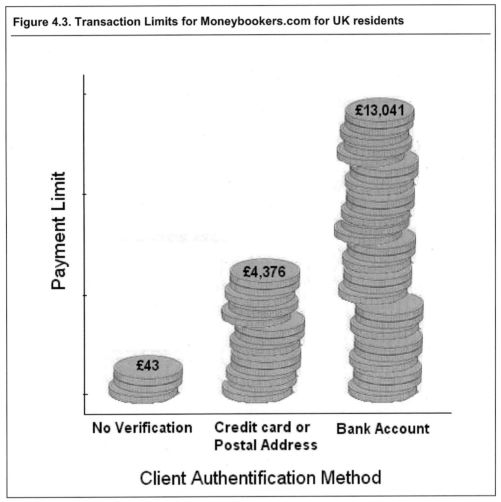

Figure 4.3. Transaction Limits for Moneybookers.com for UK residents

Source: www.Moneybookers.com.

Summary

General

There is little evidence that Internet banking presents any new or greater risk of being vulnerable to criminal abuse other than fraud, which as noted above, is being tackled by the industry itself as fraud directly affects its business. Discussions with stakeholders indicate that it presents challenges much the same as more conventional means of banking. Customer activity profiling, monitoring, and identification procedures all seem much the same as those already implemented for walk-in service at a bank branch. The non-face-to-face account opening process usually verifies the client through information provided by a centralized database. For instance, in the United States—by far the largest market for Internet banking—users are required to give their date of birth, social security number and other information that is used for verification in addition to other requirements that may be enhanced due to the non-face-to-face relationship between the bank and the online user.

Online payments may pose a challenge to governments intending to ensure all financial institutions are instituting measures to protect their business from criminal use. As detailed above, this can be the case for nonbank entities facilitating transactions through the Internet but also because incorporating such entities into the AML/CFT regime will not always be enough. The fact that Internet-based transactions can be facilitated by financial institutions outside the jurisdiction of both the sender and recipient of a funds transfer makes international cooperation ever more vital. Bilateral and multilateral efforts should be made to determine supervisory authority over these entities to ensure they are overseen and mitigating the risks of abuses such as terrorist financing.[16]

The FATF notes that an effective global effort for AML/CFT online banking and payment systems regulation demands international coordination.[17] This means that governments should work to make AML/CFT rules as similar as possible in regulating these systems to avoid, as described previously, relatively weak jurisdictions providing a regulatory "hole" that could be abused for criminal purposes.

On the other hand, it is also critical that the imposition of a regulatory regime on these services not be seen as stifling business or economic development objectives. This can best be done through a risk-based approach. The first step in this direction is to determine the actual level of risk a service poses.

We have already some clues as to the level of vulnerability the market may have to abuse. For instance, through measuring the proportion of money lost to online fraud, a crime common to criminals including terrorist financiers, the risk of abuse seems low. It has actually shrunk[18] from 3.6 percent of total online revenue in 2000 to only 1.4 percent in 2007. This suggests that as the Internet-based transaction business has grown, criminal attempts to abuse it have been increasingly less successful. Some observers have attributed this decline to the mitigation measures being taken by the Internet financial institutions themselves. Yet, it is important to note that the total amount of revenue lost has actually increased due to the growth of the market so even though the proportion has dropped, significant sums continue to be lost every year.

Terrorist Financing

There is no evidence in the research to indicate that online payments and banking poses any new threat of terrorist financing. In fact no major cases of it have been discovered by the author at the time of publishing. Both require at least some regular interface with the formal financial sector; even Internet payments usually require a bank account to make the initial deposit and to verify ID against fraud attempts. It seems very unlikely that either service would be attractive to terrorists any more than other methods of transferring value.

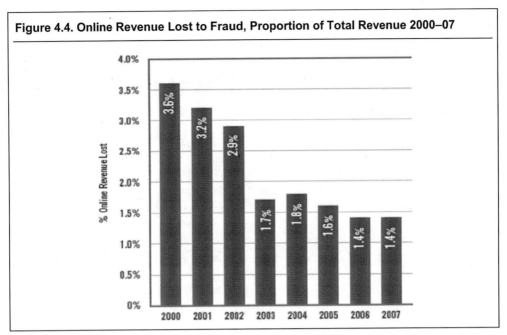

Figure 4.4. Online Revenue Lost to Fraud, Proportion of Total Revenue 2000–07

Source: Cybersource 2008.

Notes

[1] Gross 2007.

[2] See FATF 2008.

[3] CNNMoney 2008.

[4] For example, city of birth or favorite book title.

[5] Tower Group 2007

[6] Although it recently registered in Europe as a banking institution to gain greater flexibility in its services.

[7] See https://www.paypal-media.com/aboutus.cfm.

[8] See Paypal press releases at www.paypal.com.

[9] According to Paypal customer service, March 24, 2008.

[10] See FATF 2008.

[11] Holohan 2006.

[12] UN Counter Terrorism Implementation Task Force 2009a.

[13] FATF 2008.

[14] "Riskier jurisdictions" varies by provider and are usually determined based on a list provided by the government. For example in the United States, the OFAC list is common. Some providers met in fieldwork supplement it with private search databases such as World Check.

[15] www.moneybookers.com.

[16] UN Counter Terrorism Implementation Task Force 2009a.

[17] FATF 2008.

[18] Cybersource 2008.

CHAPTER 5

Digital Currency

Distinct from other online banking and Internet payment systems, there exist non-government-based currencies that are becoming more known online. Digital currency—also known as digital precious metal[1] because its value is linked to a valuable commodity such as gold or even mobile phone airtime minutes—is exchanged between account holders of the service. Given that the currency is based on the value of a commodity, its price fluctuates independently. Perhaps the most well-known of such services is e-gold Ltd., which has nearly 4.5 million open accounts based in gold, silver, platinum, and palladium[2] and at its height of success, had over US$5 million in fund transfers a day.[3]

Digital currencies usually require two intermediaries when cashing-in or cashing-out to a national currency. Users acquire the currency through a dealer who maintains an account of digital currency on behalf of the user. The dealer acquires this currency through an exchange that takes national currency for digital currency and vice versa. For example, a user in any part of the world could send Swiss francs to a dealer in another country who, for a fee, communicates with the exchange. The exchange then converts the francs into commodity ownership based on the spot rate. The same occurs for cashing-out. The dealer transacts through the exchange to convert the commodity into a national currency for the account holder. The exchange makes the conversion based on the spot rate.

After the digital currency is acquired, most systems give users the ability to transfer it without the use of intermediaries. This means that settlement is instantaneous. Some even allow the user to immediately physically retrieve the precious metal upon which the digital currency is based.[4] The simultaneous settlement makes digital currency transactions inherently riskier to criminal abuse than other methods of transferring value. Without account monitoring and transaction records (neither of which are required for this channel to function), criminal financial activities can occur anonymously, across borders and literally without a trace. It poses a risk beyond that of cash transactions because the customers are not burdened by the physical movement of funds as it occurs electronically.[5]

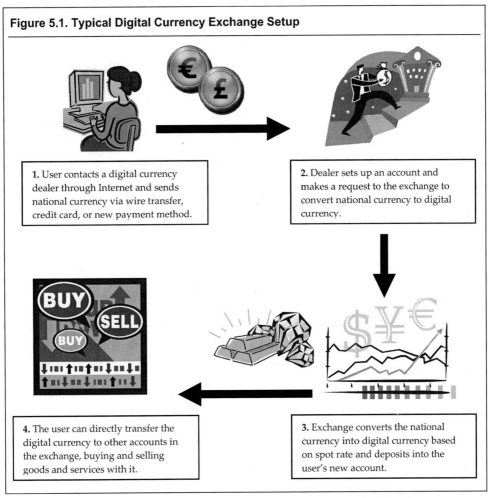

Figure 5.1. Typical Digital Currency Exchange Setup

1. User contacts a digital currency dealer through Internet and sends national currency via wire transfer, credit card, or new payment method.

2. Dealer sets up an account and makes a request to the exchange to convert national currency to digital currency.

4. The user can directly transfer the digital currency to other accounts in the exchange, buying and selling goods and services with it.

3. Exchange converts the national currency into digital currency based on spot rate and deposits into the user's new account.

Source: Based on research of e-gold Ltd. and other digital precious metal, and FATF 2006.

However, perhaps more than all other new technologies, digital currencies hold the greatest risk of not being properly regulated. This is due to the general lack of awareness among policy makers and the legal ambiguity surrounding them.[6] e-Gold, discussed below, claimed until recently that it was neither a legally defined financial institution nor a money-service business and therefore is free from the legislation regulating such entities.[7] This again brings the same problems as those mentioned in other new payment methods such as Internet banking and m-FS: providers are unevenly implementing mitigation measures for terrorist financing. This lack of regulation has made such systems vulnerable to abuse.

Just as some Alternative Remittance Systems such as Hawala[8] do not always require the typical CDD measures implemented in banks, there is a similarity with digital currency systems. This has prompted concern that this new payment method may pose an elevated risk, beyond that of falling outside the regulatory regime.[9] The fact that digital currencies are based on the value of precious metals could cause criminal organizations to move toward them as a preferred means of transferring money.[10]

In fact, they already have. e-Gold and its operator pleaded guilty to charges that they engaged in money laundering and operated an unlicensed money transmitting business. The company generally did not take any measures to defend against financial crime. According to the charges,[11] e-Gold staff were often aware of criminal abuse and refused to respond appropriately. They even noted the types of crime that their customers conducted. For instance, that a client was involved in credit card fraud, child sexual exploitation, or swindling. The fact that the Internet is ubiquitous allowed e-Gold to pretend it was located abroad while all staff and computers were based in Florida. It therefore obliged law enforcement to serve court summons to an address in Bermuda when it was truly in the United States. After just a few years of operation, it became a *modus operandi* to transfer illegal funds anonymously, offering much of the benefits of cash but without its physical limitations.

Summary

The international nature of digital currency systems demands the oversight of far more than a single national authority. This has been suggested by numerous studies, including a UN report[12] that specifically mentions digital currencies as vulnerable to the risk of lacking proper oversight. Since they are inherently multi-jurisdictional, governments should look toward developing criteria for determining supervisory responsibility.

That these systems are generally not subject to the oversight does not always imply that they do not comply with some AML/CFT standards. One digital currency provider, for example, requires certified identification documents for certain account sizes.[13] It claims that this is to (1) protect the customers' interests and (2) be compliant with regulations on money laundering. This could be a signal that, as noted about m-FS above, AML/CFT measures do not conflict with good business practices.

Terrorist Financing

The fact that digital currency systems are unregulated and more vulnerable to criminal abuse has been supported by media reports from Europe in which a prospective terrorist apparently demanded a ransom payment through digital currency.[14] Yet, except for that single incident, no case of terrorist financing and digital currencies are known to the author.

This may be an indication that digital currencies are not particularly more attractive to terrorist financing activities than any other crime. Closing the general criminal vulnerabilities in digital currencies seems likely to make them less attractive to terrorist financiers as well. The demise of e-Gold due to its complicity in criminal endeavors may begin a broader effort by governments to regulate these systems and raise awareness of their existence.

Notes

[1] This term is used by FATF.

[2] According to its website at www.e-gold.com

[3] Condon 2008.

[4] e-dinar for instance. See www.e-dinar.com.

[5] The U.S. Treasury notes that these systems are also more attractive to criminals because the instant settlement gives users security that the payment is carried through so they are not swindled.

[6] World Bank fieldwork, 2008.

[7] Business Week 2006a.

[8] Vaccani 2009.

[9] World Bank fieldwork, 2008.

[10] e-dinar, for example, is a spin-off of e-gold. It is specifically aimed at Muslims wanting to pay alms (zakat) or make transfers of money that is backed by *physical* gold or silver. See https://www.e-dinar.com/html/1_4.html.

[11] United States of America vs e-Gold, Ltd.; Gold & Silver Reserve, Inc.; Douglas L. Jackson; Barry K. Downey; and Reid A. Jackson. Crim. No. 07-109 (RMC) April 2008.

[12] UN Counter Terrorism Implementation Task Force 2009a.

[13] e-dinar requires all accounts that are larger than US$1,000 to have certified identity documents. The quality of its verification and monitoring procedures have not been assessed for the purposes of this report. See https://www.e-dinar.com/html/4_7.html

[14] Business Week 2006b.

CHAPTER 6

Conclusions

In all the major types of new payment methods discussed—value cards, the online banking and payments, digital currencies and mobile telephones—the uncertainty for market players on what they are obligated to do to close their terrorist financing risks is the outstanding issue. Some of these channels present unique risks of being attractive for general criminal abuse, including terrorist financing because they often have an ambiguous place in the legal regime. Furthermore, it is certain that even newer financial systems will emerge and existing ones will continue to evolve rapidly. Research indicates policy makers are not moving fast enough to bring the new types of financial institutions described above into the regulatory umbrella.

New Technologies, New Risks of Terrorist Financing?

At the same time, it is important to recognize how vulnerable such channels really are to abuse by terrorists. The risks of the new payment methods described in this paper seem far more relevant to broader financial crimes—such as money laundering and fraud—than specifically to terrorist financing. Although terrorist financiers have been known to use such illicit activities to fund their operations, the new technologies described here seem not to have been any more attractive than more traditional means to move money. Indeed, none of the risks in the technologies described in this paper are unique to terrorist financing, a key point that must be considered by policy makers when wrestling with the issue of overseeing these channels. More work should be done to outline the vulnerabilities to other types of crime that these technologies may have.

Falling Outside the Law

Many new payment methods can be vulnerable to anonymity risks by the lack of proper customer due diligence requirements, a base for any successful AML/CFT system. This deficiency is often the result of the provider falling outside the regulatory regime. For instance, in the case of mobile financial services, the telecom provider may not be required by law to specifically carry out the same KYC procedures required of traditional financial institutions such as banks. Another example is the risk that digital currency will not fall under any regulatory regime at all, leaving both the service and the provider completely alone in determining what measures, if any, are in place to mitigate the risks of abuse, including that of anonymity.

Table 5.1. Payment Methods and Risks of Abuse

	Market Status	Criminal Risk Summary	Terrorist Financing Observations
Value Cards	Some kinds are growing, others declining.	Has some criminal advantages over cash but simple controls can mitigate.	Not particularly vulnerable.
Mobile Financial Services	Booming, especially in Asia and Africa.	Typical business model is setup in a way that reduces attractiveness to criminals.	Not particularly vulnerable.
Online Banking/ Payments	Growing, especially in advanced economies.	Risk of fraud could be higher than other channels but industry has strong interest to tackle this.	Not particularly vulnerable.
Digital Currencies	Shrinking since conviction and freezing of accounts of market leader.	Customer anonymity and no transaction traceability that are intrinsic to many business models have shown to be attractive to criminal activity. Also, supervisory jurisdiction is unclear as transactions take place over the Internet in non-national currencies.	General criminal risk but not particular to terrorist financing.

Source: Author.

It is important that governments work to close this gap by identifying the financial channels and players in their markets and developing a legal structure that is inclusive of all. One way to ensure that no service or provider is left out of the law is for authorities to conduct regular surveys of the market which is already being done in some countries. A second possibility is for the law to set broad principles for players, of any type, so that innovators are not discouraged by legal ambiguity and AML/CFT responsibilities are clearly assigned.

Intersection of Industries an Opportunity

Often new technological methods of making transactions intersect. This can be seen in the recent emergence of mobile money, which is a type of digital currency accessible through mobile telephones. Still being discussed by industry, this mobile-accessible digital currency could be based in airtime credits or other form of tender, separate from a national currency. Rather than providing reason for alarm, the move to deal with them should be seen as an opportunity for governments and industry players to exchange information on best-practices in regulation.

Governments should be aware of the players and the services that exist in the market to determine whether to regulate and, if so, to what extent. New payment channels must have some link to the conventional financial system so fund transfers between channels (for example, a deposit from a traditional bank account to a digital currency account or vice versa) are an opportunity for governments to identify new payment systems. This will then allow them to perform a market assessment to identify the financial services provided, the entities providing them and what their risks are, if any.

Coordination with and within the Private Sector

Regulation is best done in collaboration with industry. Fieldwork[1] into some new payment methods suggests that the most effective regulatory regime is one that is carefully crafted with the market players themselves. This ensures that loopholes are closed while also facilitating a sustainable, pro-business environment. Discussions with industry on the development of new technologies are particularly important in light of the fast-paced evolution of existing technologies and rapid emergence of new ones. The new payment methods described here are likely to someday change or be made obsolete by even newer ones so governments should regularly consult industry to learn of market developments and thus remain alert to any new vulnerability to terrorist financing.

Past experience indicates that discussions with industry are most effective when authorities give stakeholders' input serious attention when designing such regulations. This will strengthen the public-private coordination and help make sure that government is quickly informed of the rapid adjustments in the market. A regular forum between the two is often an effective means to do this.[2]

Several governments have disclosed information on the nature of innovative payment businesses in their markets. This information suggests that, when laws allow it, data sharing amongst financial service providers themselves empowers the private sector to fight financial crime. The FATF suggests that commercial websites and Internet payment providers be encouraged to exchange data on transactions to mitigate risk.

International Effort

Some new payment methods go far beyond the reach of national authorities and therefore require authorities in different countries to work in concert. This is especially the case for digital currencies and other Internet-based transaction services in which various functions of the provider are separated among several jurisdictions. How to best establish such coordination, whether it requires a new multilateral agency or a strengthening of existing ones, remains an issue for consideration.

Policy makers should explore the best way to move forward on international cooperation and coordination as recommended by the FATF. Online banking and Internet payments as well as digital currencies represent channels where this is particularly relevant. The ubiquity of the Internet can enable noncompliant providers or terrorists to avoid AML/CFT controls of one jurisdiction while still transferring funds. This can only be mitigated by collaboration both in terms of making the regimes similar as well as support for investigations.

Awareness Raising Is Key

Efforts should be redoubled to raise awareness of the existence, risks, and effective mitigations measures for these channels. Some of the governments that were informally approached for this work were unaware that some new payment systems were operating—or even based their global business—in their jurisdiction. To build an effective regime requires government knowledge of the service. This can best be done by providers notifying the government before they enter the market.

Furthermore, greater guidance should be provided so that governments can best take advantage of the economic opportunities brought by new technologies while mitigating the risk of terrorist financing. It is hoped that this report has contributed to this discussion, bringing to light new issues and prompting deeper research into them.

Notes

[1] Chatain et al. 2008.
[2] UN Counter Terrorism Implementation Task Force 2009a.

References

Acharya, Arabinda 2008. Consortium for Combating the Financing of Terrorism Conference. Singapore.

Business Week. 2006a. "Dr. Jackson's Golden Vision Investigative Reports." January 9. http://www.businessweek.com/magazine/content/06_02/b3966105.htm.

———. 2006b. "Gold Rush." Investigative Reports. January 9. http://www.businessweek.com/magazine/content/06_02/b3966094.htm.

Chatain, Pierre; Raul Hernandez-Coss, Kamil Borowik, and Andrew Zerzan. 2008. *Integrity in Mobile Phone Financial Services*. Washington, DC: World Bank.

CNNMoney. 2008. "BankWest Selects Omniture to Drive Online Customer Banking Services." 17 March. http://money.cnn.com/news/newsfeeds/articles/marketwire/0376019.htm.

Condon, Stephanie. 2008. "Judge spares E-Gold Directors Jail Time." *CNET News*. November 20. http://news.cnet.com/8300-13578_3-38-0.html?keyword=gold (Accessed 14 May 2009).

Committee on Payment and Settlement Systems (CPSS). 2003. *Glossary of Terms Used in Payments and Settlement Systems*. Bank for International Settlements. March. http://www.bis.org/publ/cpss00b.htm.

Cybersource. 2008. *9th Annual Online Fraud Report*. Online payment fraud trends, merchant practices and benchmarks. http://www.scribd.com/doc/305122/2007-Online-Credit-Card-Fraud-Report.

Deloitte and Touche. 2007 "Gift Cards, Money Laundering, and Fraud: Protecting Against the Perfect Holiday Storm." Consumer Business Webcast. 13 December. Speakers include: David Gilles, Stacy Janiak, Brian Midkiff and John Scheffler.

Demetis, Dionysios S., and Bernard W. Dyer. 2006. Paper Interview. London School of Economics, Department of Management, Information Systems Group. http://personal.lse.ac.uk/demetis/PaperInterview.pdf (accessed 20 August 2007).

E-dinar Ltd. 2009. Public Website. http://www.e-dinar.com.

E-gold Ltd. 2009. Public Website. http://e-gold.com/.

Ehrenfeld, Rachel, and John Wood. 2007. "Terrorist Funding in Real Time." *American Thinker*. April 11, 2007. http://www.americanthinker.com/2007/04/terrorist_funding_in_real_time.html (accessed August 20, 2007).

European Committee for Banking Standards. 2003. *Overview of European Electronic Purse Products*. Version 4.0. September. http://www.ecbs.org/Download/TR102v4.PDF.

Evaluation Partnership Limited. 2006. *Evaluation of the E-Money Directive (2000/46/EC) Final Report*. February 17. European Commission. http://ec.europa.eu/internal_market/bank/docs/e-money/evaluation_en.pdf.

Financial Action Task Force on Money Laundering and Terrorist Financing. 2006. *Report on New Payment Methods*. 13 October. United Nations.

———. 2008. *Money Laundering & Terrorist Financing Vulnerabilities of Commercial Websites and Internet Payment Systems*. 18 June. United Nations.

Furletti, Mark. 2004. *Prepaid Card Markets & Regulation. Discussion Paper*. Federal Reserve Bank of Philadelphia. Payments Cards Center. February. http://www.philadelphiafed.org/pcc/papers/2004/Prepaid_022004.pdf.

Gross, Grant. 2007. "Congress Votes to Extend Internet Tax Ban." *PCWorld Magazine,* October 31.

GSM Association. 2006. "GSM Hits Two Billion Milestone." Press Release. June

———. 2008. "Mobile Financial Services to Thrive with Right Regulation" Press Release. February 6.

Holohan, Cathering. 2006. *Policing Online Money Laundering*. November 6. http://www.businessweek.com/technology/content/nov2006/tc20061106_986949. htm.

International Telecommunications Union. 2007. *Global Trends in Telecommunications*.

Mas, Ignacio and Sarah Rotman. 2008. *Going Cashless at the Point of Sale: Hits and Misses in Developed Countries*. Consultative Group to Assist the Poor (CGAP). December. World Bank, Washington, DC.

Moneybookers Group. 2008. Public Website and User Signup. March. www.moneybookers.com.

National Branded Prepaid Card Association (NBPCA). 2007. *AML Best Practices Summary For Issuers of Network Branded Prepaid Cards*. August. http://www.nbpca.com/docs/AML-BP-Summary.pdf.

Paypal Media. 2009. *About Us*. San Jose, California. https://www.paypal-media.com/aboutus.cfm.

Paypal Services. 2008. Fieldwork conference call. March 7.

Scheffler, John. 2007. U.S. Assurance Leader, Retail, Deloitte & Touche USA LLP. Fieldwork conference call. December.

Western Union. 2007. "Western Union and GSMA to Create New Global Mobile Money Transfer Service." Press Release. October. http://ir.westernunion.com/press/releaseDetail.cfm?ReleaseID=269902.

Vaccani, Matteo. 2009. "Alternative Remittance Systems and Terrorism Financing: Risks and Mitigation Strategies." World Bank, Washington, DC.

World Bank. 2007a. *Finance for All? Policies and Pitfalls in Expanding Access*. Policy Research Report. Washington, DC: World Bank. August.

World Bank. 2007b. "Next Generation Access to Finance: Gaining Scale and Reducing Costs with Technology and Credit Scoring". Conference. September 17-19. Washington DC.

Yingling, Edward L. (President of American Banker's Association). April 26, 2007. Testimony to the Subcommittee on Financial Institutions and Consumer Credit Financial Services Committee United States House of Representatives. http://www.house.gov/apps/list/hearing/financialsvcs_dem/htyingling042607.pdf.

United Nations Counter Terrorism Implementation Task Force. 2009a. *Report on Tackling the Financing of Terrorism*. United Nations. http://www.un.org/terrorism/pdfs/ wg5-financing.pdf.

————. 2009b. Working Group on Tackling the Financing of Terrorism. 2009. Round table discussion with intelligence agents. Vienna.

United States District Court for the District of Columbia. 2008. *United States of America VS E-GOLD Ltd.; Gold & Silerver Reserve, Inc.; Douglas L. Jackson; Barry K. Downey; and Reid A. Jackson*. Crim. No. 07-109 (RMC) April.

Eco-Audit

Environmental Benefits Statement

The World Bank is committed to preserving Endangered Forests and natural resources. We print World Bank Working Papers and Country Studies on postconsumer recycled paper, processed chlorine free. The World Bank has formally agreed to follow the recommended standards for paper usage set by Green Press Initiative—a nonprofit program supporting publishers in using fiber that is not sourced from Endangered Forests. For more information, visit www.greenpressinitiative.org.

In 2008, the printing of these books on recycled paper saved the following:

Trees*	Solid Waste	Water	Net Greenhouse Gases	Total Energy
355	16,663	129,550	31,256	247 mil.
*40 feet in height and 6–8 inches in diameter	Pounds	Gallons	Pounds CO_2 Equivalent	BTUs

green press
INITIATIVE